W9-CTQ-288

WHAT REMAINS

Charles Entrekin

Cover photograph by Charles Klein
Cover design by Tyler Varian-Gonzalez

Copyright © 2020 Charles Entrekin

ISBN: 978-1-7337025-9-1

All rights reserved. No part of this book may be used or
reproduced in any manner whatsoever without written
permission, except in the case of quotes for personal use and
brief quotations embedded in critical articles or reviews.

Poetic Matrix Press
www.poeticmatrix.com

WHAT REMAINS

Acknowledgements

This manuscript would not have been possible without the advice, suggestions, and encouragement about structure and composition from my assistant, Heidi Varian. I owe her a great debt for constant attention to detail about line breaks, choice, and placement of poems. And great thanks, as ever, to my beautiful wife Gail, who helped organize and edit the final manuscript.

Aura, Canary: *The Fish Found in Her Dream*
Baltic Avenue: *To a Child in the Rain*
Berkeley Poets Workshop & Press: *Alabama Kudzu; All Pieces of a Legacy; Ballad; Birmingham; Creek Song; Dink; For a Girl I Once Knew* (now *"Sena"*)*; January, the Day You Died; Let's Play a Game; Parting; The Large and Small of It; The Photograph is Wrong.*
California Quarterly: *Roots*
Kudzu: *In Birmingham*
Louisville Review: *Alabama in December, April in Alabama, Flashback, Leaving Alabama*
Nimrod: *At Hearst Street House, Grandmother Allison's Stance*
New Southerner: *One Day at a Time*
Northwest Poetry Review: *Yes*
Pinch Penny Press: *Report from Thomas, Ten Years after the Accident; Fourteen Reasons Why; Riverside, Alabama*
San Diego Poetry Annual: *New Year's Day, 1983*
Tunnel Road: *1941*
West Branch: *A Day's Work*

Charles Entrekin's previously published books in which these poems appear:

Casting for the Cutthroat (Thunder City Press, 1977): *Night-song, Thoughts from a Plane Over Birmingham.*

All Pieces of a Legacy (BPW&P, 1975): *Here in the Dark, Love; Awakening.*

Listening: New and Selected Works (Poetic Matrix Press, 2010): ALL ABOVE TITLES except *Roots; At Hearst Street House; Grandmother Allison's Stance; Here in the Dark, Love.*

Contents

WHAT REMAINS

Mise En Scene:
Setting the Stage

Creek Song   1
Hay Stacker   2
An Alabama Song   4
To a Child in the Rain   5
Roots   6
The Fox in the Woods   7
Seasons   9

Apples Bursting Among the Leaves:
Stories We Tell Ourselves

Okra   13
1941   14
Building the Atlanta Highway, 1948   15
Early Portrait of my Father   18
Marvin   20
Yes   22
All Pieces of a Legacy   24
Ballad   25
The First Television   26
Forbidden Visit   31
The Large and Small of It   36
A Day's Work   37
Choices   38
In Birmingham   40
A Man   41

Let's Play a Game   43
Grandmother Allison's Stance   44
Parting   46

Non-Recouvrable: Unsalvageable
For Janice Kirkpatrick Entrekin
(1943-1966)

Riverside, Alabama   49
Holding the Invisible   50
The Promised Land   51
Night Song   52
After a Fight   53
Ophelia's Dream, 1963   54
The Photograph is Wrong   56
Here in the Dark, Love   57
This Unfinished Dream   58
Alabama Kudzu   59
Advantage   60
Asylum   61
To Remember You   62
Fourteen Reasons Why   63
The Fish Found in Her Dream   65
Alabama Night Walk   66

The Meaning of Escape

Alabama Politics   71
Leaving Alabama   74
Report from Thomas, Ten Years After the Accident   76
For Sena   77
Letter from My Father   78
Dear Jordi (Tuscaloosa, Alabama)   80
Birmingham   82

Desert-Wrecked Dreamer:
California

One Day at a Time   85
High, All-night Driving to Berkeley   86
Flashback   87
At Hearst Street House   89
January, the Day You Died   90
November in Berkeley   91
New Year's Day, 1983   92
What the Woman Said in my Dream   93
Thoughts from a Plane over Birmingham   94

Renouvellement:
Renewal

Alabama in December   97
Dink   99
All that Remains is Her Inlaid Mozart Music Box   100
April in Alabama   103
Postcard View, Panama City   105
Drucilla   106
Last Parting   108
Azaleas   109
Renewal   110

Author Biography

To my brothers and sisters,
Marvin, Betty Ann, Stephen, David, and Cindy,
who shared the joys and terrors of our growing up together.

Mise En Scene:
Setting the Stage

Creek Song

*T*he innocence of my childhood
stalks me. Down through my grandfather's woods
it winds like his creek through the soft Southern forest.
It is alive with moccasin-mouthed shadows,
with rock-creek sounds of decaying wood,
with the log bridge beneath me soughing,
whispering, Be still, be still, be still...

Hay Stacker

*T*oo small to lift a pitchfork full
from below, I would climb up top and catch each throw,
midair, then guide and drop the load in one motion
until the wagon would hold no more.
          Then coming out of the dust from the back four acres,
I'd be atop the hay, barely able to breathe in the heat,
yet lying back in the wet of my own sweat, almost complete.
          And when we passed beneath the big pear tree
there in the middle of my grandfather's pasture,
I knew how it would be:
I would stick out my hand and
take the pear straight out of the air
without effort; it would come to me
because it belonged to me.
          I hadn't yet guessed how things could go wrong,
or how it might be to be left alone, or that one
could lose badly and go down at the end
like my mother, shaking and defeated.
          I was, in that moment, simply there
watching my cousins and uncles in the distance, shimmering
in the hot air like mirages in black rubber boots
with pitchforks in hand,
          and when I took my first dusty bite,
          it was like my first
sinking deep into a woman's body,
almost overwhelming, and I could feel

the pear's juice sinking into me
as I lay there in the hay-scented air, adrift
and becoming everything around me,
    until suddenly I laughed out loud
    without knowing
what the laughter was about
as it poured out of me
at the top of the tree-high stack
while the future waited,
and I was carried on the harvest to the barn.

An Alabama Song

In every direction a creek
and mosquitoes. You stand on a promontory
above a lake, a Southern swamp
of drowned trees, and leap

      starkly naked out into space,
grab hold of a knot on a rope,
and swing into that joy of recklessness,
a teenager in full flight, flying

      down the bright, sharp-edged rock face,
leaving everything behind in a rush of fear
before you break free and begin to rise,
up into your own weightlessness,

      where your body floats in a sky-blue day
as you push away from the knotted rope
and stop for a moment, going nowhere,
a moment when you have let go

      because you know how to begin the fall,
know how to slip into that slow-motion roll
of a perfect dive, leave no splash at all, and
enter that soft wet mesh of forgetfulness.

To a Child in the Rain

It was to play in the rain
you took off your clothes,
damned the gutter's river,
Red Mountain's water down Birmingham
streets, the way you could lie back
and be carried away, naked,
in the wet wash of summer rain,
and no plans but to swim down the river,
your street, become the world you lived in,
the fire tower and mountain top,
the mimosa and oak, as if the horizon
could reach down and touch you
like a sweeping brush stroke,
and you belonged to the landscape,
like sidewalk cracks and mud, the way
the tiny glass horses you held
remained rearing and alive
in their milky white light.

Roots

Roots in Clay County, Alabama,
sticking out of the ground
like hard old men who've made up their minds,
set their grip hard against everything
young and swift.

When I walk out across this piece of earth
all covered over with honeysuckle and weeds,
the ground seems to suck at my feet
as though it were alive
and needed me
holding soil in place,
replacing stumps falling into rot.

The Fox in the Woods
Springville, Alabama

My grandfather used to tell me
about the animals in the woods on his land
but I could never see them.
Be quiet, he advised, *and you'll see them.*
Then one day, my grandfather whispered
to me it was time—
I should go down into the woods
to the old logging bridge, to see
if the forest creatures would speak to me.
Be still, he said, *Sit for half an hour
in silence. Listen.*

Seeking shade from the sun, I sat
on pine duff and vines and leaned back
against a fallen old oak, green with moss.
Creek water was whispering over rocks,
water striders crossed over the current.
I counted long minutes.

Out of the quiet, a turtle's mottled head
popped the surface of the creek,
sank down as a rabbit came out of the weeds,
froze, fidgeted, and hopped away.
A flying squirrel leapt, tree to tree,
floated like a ghost
past the perch of a yellow-headed finch.

And then a fox walked right up to me—
a red fox, ears perked, tail down, lips back, grinning.
He stopped three steps in front of me.
At first, I remembered how my grandmother
once shot and killed a rabid dog.
I thought, *Don't move, be invisible.*

But then I felt recognized
as we looked into each other's eyes,
part of the same world, this forest.
An acceptance flowed through me—
he belonged here
and I belonged in the same space,
joined.
I wanted to touch him
and I reached out my hand.
There was no fear.
But my hand had ruptured the tension
that held us together.
I knew at once I had violated
some barrier between us.
A twig snapped,
he leapt away,
he was gone,
and I was alone,
no longer part of the forest.

Seasons

Once the sky was blue, so blue
it seemed you could throw rocks into it
and they would not come to earth.
You would never be held accountable,
could run amok in the cornfields,
break the planned order,
run so far into your anger that dying
meant nothing, meant only a river,
a flood always leaving the land
richer for its coming.
      It was your age of seasons,
nothing but being young, when everything
had its own place, could come and go
to return like the seasons;
and you could fall through space
as on a cardboard ride down,
before the highways were made,
before the day your dog tried to cross
and you continued on, unable to stop
seeing things break that could not be replaced.
      In the absence of seasons
healing happens all at once,
like a flowering no one sees,
like a plant that blooms only once
in the desert at midnight under moonlight,
and you are kneeling in the midst of kisses
where the pale arms of a lover heal all wounds.

Apples Bursting Among the Leaves:
Stories We Tell Ourselves

Okra

*D*eracinated African vegetable
its tough green prickly pods
and the ache in its spiky hairs
surviving in the sunbaked earth
and Southern summer rains
and the red clay dirt

in the calloused hands that gather it in
day in and day out
that have measured its hurt and found it
worth bearing

for the taste, rolled in
corn meal, cooked in Crisco,
cut, pickled, boiled, fried

and the women are removing their aprons
and the men are stepping from their Chevrolets
these heavy-bodied people
who understand
the nature of okra,
who have taken it in
and made it their own.

1941

Arriving in the parking lot
the evening I'm born, he stands,
hands in his empty pockets,
fresh from a high school
that never taught him anything
about anything, except fighting
and the war going on,
and knows that green sea of wall lockers
is behind him. It is August
and the black pavement still steams
with rain. Staring up
the high brick wall and windows,
he tries to guess which one I'm in,
not yet believing there is one,
those square yellow lights like sleep
and a dream he can't wake up from.

Building the Atlanta Highway, 1948

Somebody showed it to me
and I found it by myself.
Lew Welch

When they made the initial cuts for the Birmingham-to-Atlanta Highway, it sliced right through our forest, our street, and our imaginations, and changed our neighborhood forever. The woods we had played in would never be the same. Instead of a tangled brown and green forest that went on forever, our playground became steep banks of raw red earth. These banks were part of the cut that framed a mystical straight line of iron rich dirt destined to become a superhighway to Atlanta. This man-made line extended out and over the horizon, curving into infinity. It looked like a long red scratch exposing the skin of the planet.

The building of the Atlanta Highway had a powerful effect on us kids. It was as if the Roman Empire had sent men and machines to make a road through our village. Suddenly the manifest power of the government was amongst us. They took away the forest but left behind giant toys. Every day, every chance we got, for a whole year, we neighborhood kids, after the workers had left for the day, swarmed barefoot down over the hillside and ran to play amongst the tractors and caterpillars and earthmovers.

With curiosities larger than fear, we plunged in and walked about in wonder amongst those massive machines, entranced by the garage-sized mud puddles of rich red clay, the smells of blackened wicks in their stinking smoke pots, the huge off-white boulders raised up like prehistoric creatures rolled over onto their sides, asleep.

In the gloaming of early evening shadows and Southern summer heat, we crept over the snake-like, black cables, thicker than our arms, and played war games.

In the daytime, the giant yellow machines belonged to the Empire. In the evening, they were ours.

We also discovered something else late into that summer. A neighborhood, once concealed from us by the impenetrable forest, now suddenly stood revealed. Kids we'd never seen before simply appeared in the middle of our games. Black kids. They were also crawling in and around those giant yellow bulldozers and earthmovers.

Black kids were different from us somehow, but we didn't know what that difference was supposed to be. No one had ever said. We didn't know if we should play with them or not. So we did.

We threw mud balls at them.

They threw mud balls at us.

We reorganized our games around a new idea—it was their neighborhood against ours. We became neighborhood armies with reconnaissance teams, supply lines for making and delivering mud balls, and then we made forays into each other's territory in surprise attacks.

This went on for weeks.

We began to know each other's names, laugh, and wave, before going home to our mothers and dinner.

For a while, we lived in the easy regularity of friend-ships that comes from a close-knit neighborhood. After sup-per, with the crickets and tree frogs calling out their mating signals in the sweltering dusk, the calls would go out, and our friends—new and old—would rush over to our house. Then, sitting together inside a screened-in front porch, we'd drink

iced tea, play Canasta, and listen to the evening radio pro-
grams—"The Lone Ranger," "The Shadow," "The Fat Man,"
"The Green Hornet," "Mr. and Mrs. North"—until finally some-
one's mom would begin calling and we would have to break up.

Then, lying in bed, the quiet was accompanied by my
brother's rhythmic breathing. I would listen out the window
to the lawn sprinklers hissing over the grass as June bugs
crashed. I watched the death's head moths flutter in the
porchlight, flapping their wings hard, getting burned, and
then clinging to the screens just outside my bedroom window.

Amongst the night sounds, I strained to hear the lilting
voice of my mother and the low, clipped tones of my father
out on the porch, talking about us kids. They debated our
young friends, our new games.

For a brief moment in time, we lived in an integrated
neighborhood. Then one day we moved out of the city into
the rural suburbs, away from the progress of the highway,
away from the earthmovers, and left our neighborhood and
our friends behind.

Early Portrait of My Father

East Lake, Alabama, 1950

*H*e worked for Southern Bell
as a telephone cable repairman.
He wore a dark green uniform with gold lettering.
He worked nine-to-five
and sometimes nights.
The phone call would come
during storms
and he would go
for the time-and-a-half money,
double on Sundays.

He could repair anything:
bicycles, lawnmowers, cars, trucks.
He had a two-hundred-pound vice
he used to bend struts.
He wore company-bought,
machine-made, precision-steel scissors
on his side, hooked to his belt—
amazing, shiny.
Those scissors could cut anything:
paper,
rubber,
band-aids.
They could
strip wire,
shape tin,

trim rose bushes,
anything.
They were so fine, they could even cut our hair.

When I saw him playing the piano,
I was surprised.
He couldn't read music,
but he could pick out a tune by ear.
I watched his swollen damaged fingers,
discolored ruined fingernails,
touching each soft ivory key
one note at a time,
handsome face cocked and listening.
And I could hear the tune
slowly, erratically, come into my head.
Ruby lips above the waters,
blowing bubbles soft and fine,
his calloused hands moved across the keys,
making the song come alive.

Marvin

You sat up late into the night
to listen to my stories,
even when the threat of a beating
mixed my whispers with fear—
"Be quiet in there or I'll come in with my belt!"
But you, listening, unafraid,
taught me how to go on,
knowing what it might cost.
Dad had worked all the night before.
Little David and Steve and you and me
talking on and on
in the dark
until we paid.

I remember our tears,
the smell of our bunk beds,
the odor of our tennis shoes.
The end of those nights came slowly,
when truth was in the comradery of our tears
and the long sighs of our suffering.
But we knew what the price would be
and we would pay it again and again.

You listened and I learned
how to tell a story,
stretching it out like a long-awaited drink of water,
making beginnings and endings that never held up,
but middles that ran on and on in wonderful falsifications,
our best, most lasting request before sleep.

Yes

for Aloysius Wybell (Bud) Allison

We were waiting in a stand of pines.
The hounds announced themselves.
Yes, he said, *yes,*
they'll cross over there.
And he began to run.
    I remember catching up,
my uncle taking the pistol from his clothes
as he knelt on the road.
It had rained earlier that morning
and the smoke stayed close to the ground,
the sound burning in my ears.
    Yes, he said,
fine rabbit if he doesn't have worms,
and he smiled, his hand
once again disappearing beneath his coat.
    And the rabbit was so small,
shot through the head,
and I was amazed and puzzled,
a child knowing that shot was
a feat of perfection somehow.
So small
and he had shot it from so far away.

So small, and yes,
he had stood there
holding it by the ears,
the wind bending around us,
the trees singing the song
of what could be remembered,
but never again touched.

All Pieces of a Legacy

You receive the memories, the hunger,
and the dreams, shiny as the eyes of madmen
before stately antebellum mansions,
even for the poor more than they were,
like lightning bugs stuck to a summer evening.

Patterns like footprints in the grass
of a barefooted run with a June bug
on a string, like a child hugged in the arms
of motherhood, tied to a solid, hard-backed green,
the buzzing, broken as first sex in the back of a car.

And you remember the funny talk of poontang
in barber shops before the hunt begins,
the talk of the remorseless chicken thief,
the hungry coon sought after in the night
out beyond the chinaberry tree, the mimosa
and crepe myrtle, out beyond even the dogwood,

through the kudzu, hunted and smiling
from the pine tree, smiling at the dogs
pulled with chains from the moon-cut pine.
You remember that trapped and smiling, high-up coon,
you remember the hunger that would not cease, cease.

Ballad

for Uncle Bud

He would be in the forest lifting out
his metal band-aid box, sandpaper glued to the bottom,
never carried a lighter, and the match would flare:
         the smell of pipe tobacco in the cold winter
air, and I remember him always working, planting,
fishing, walking, a man who distrusted words,
loved his dogs, who would be gone
         hunting all day with his dogs, listening
for the closing of the circle, to his best dog,
listening, leaning with his back against the mossed side,
against some dead old oak.

The First Television

That which does not kill us will make us stronger.
—Friedrich Nietzsche

My mother's twin sister Ethel and her husband, Gaither Lee (a large, red-faced man who could eat white onions raw and drink whiskey straight from the bottle), had jumped ahead of our family in importance because they had gone out and purchased their own television set. I am not sure which fact amazed us more: that there really was such a thing as "television" or that Gaither Lee and Ethel had gotten one ahead of us. And Marvin and I, ages five and seven respectively, could barely stand still because we were dazzled by the news being passed on to us by our mother. Mom had all the real information concerning family plans, destinations, and changes in status.

That summer in Birmingham, Alabama, 1949, I was standing on our screened-in front porch in the heat, suffering a starched shirt that itched, and watching Mom put her finishing touches on Betty Ann, aged four, while Dad, wearing a tie and white shirt, held Stephen Michael, nine months. We were being dressed up not because we were going to church, but because it was Sunday, and everybody else would be dressed up, and we were going over to Aunt Ethel's to see their new television set.

That year we owned a squarish, blue-gray, four-door Plymouth with brown interior, and back door handles that opened outwards by pushing down instead of pulling up. Dad, recently hired by Southern Bell Telephone as a line repairman, had just bought it. Mom still didn't know how to drive. So we were going to take our new car out for a spin on the way to see the brand new television set.

Maybe it was the excitement of the proposed visit, but more probably it was the simple animus of brothers that pushed us over into the fight that caused all the trouble. Our fights had a way of escalating beyond control. I always thought I could manage Marvin, and sometimes I could. But sometimes Marvin, without warning, would tip our disagreements over into all-out war. I think he thought I was trying to take advantage of him. So, suddenly, without warning, we would have to fight. This one was likely caused by something about sitting next to the open window in order to spit at the mailboxes at the bottom of the hill.

Well, once we got going, naturally we completely forgot about Betty Ann, who was actually the one sitting by the window. And then Marvin and I, locked up like two cats that could give no quarter, began pushing and grabbing and rolling about in the back seat. And Betty Ann, who had been sitting quietly in all innocence beside us, began to try to squirm out from under our maelstrom. I vaguely remember her new shiny black shoes and a short print dress that tied in the back as one remembers something seen but not focused on. She was four, barely human.

Anyway, Betty Ann, attempting to escape the action by slipping under our writhing forms, had leaned away from us while holding onto the door handle. We never even noticed her. I had broken loose from Marvin's grip and shoved him onto the other side of the car, even as he was still trying to catch and hold onto me, and then Betty Ann just disappeared. Somehow, as the car took a turn, the door swung open with Betty Ann holding on and then slammed closed again, and Betty Ann was gone.

Marvin and I recognized her absence almost imme-
diately. We stopped fighting and stared at each other. Then,
without a word between us, we leaped up onto the back seat
to look out the window. And there she was rolling down the
hill behind us.

Marvin and I both screamed, *"Dad!"*

For a long moment nothing seemed to happen. Then
suddenly the car lurched to a stop, and Marvin and I were
thrown backwards against the front seats. Then, in slow mo-
tion, we watched Dad leap out of the car and begin hurrying
toward Betty Ann. But halfway there, he abruptly stopped as if
he'd reached the end of an invisible string, and turned, almost
falling down, and began, face grim with determination, to
chase after us.

Our car had begun rolling forward, driverless, down
the hill. Dad had forgotten to set the emergency brake, and
Mom and Stephen Michael were screaming.

Marvin and I leaped up, wide-eyed, to watch as Betty
Ann struggled to her feet by herself and, crying out with arms
and hands extended, began to chase after Dad, who was now
chasing after us.

At the last driveway before the intersection Dad man-
aged to run along beside the careering car, jump in, pull up on
the emergency brake and then turn the wheels into the curb.
We came to a stop on a neighbor's driveway and front lawn.
Then Betty Ann caught up, and Dad was examining her in his
arms. Marvin and I became very quiet. *We might not get to
see the television.*

Back at the house, we sat on the front steps as Mom
and Dad decided what to do.

Dad said, *"Well, Ruth, what do you think? Should we
go or not?"*

As usual, it was Mom who made these final decisions. So, Mom turned and, with her, we all turned back to Betty Ann.

Mom asked her, *"How do you feel, honey?"*

There was a long quiet pause. Betty Ann looked up, her face still puffy from crying. A big bump and angry-looking scratch marks on one side of her face made her look a little sad and lopsided and she was completely dirty, except where tears had streaked down her cheeks.

"I was scared you were going to leave me."

She was going to be all right. We would get to go.

Somehow actually seeing our first television did not live up to expectations. Gaither Lee's television screen was very small with lots of black and white test patterns and a loud tuning-in signal, an electronic whistle in the middle of a white noise of static. And then it offered "The Howdy Doody Show" to all of us in their small living room, the television on one side and a large fan on the other. There were Ethel and Gaither Lee, cousin Dink in his wheelchair, slumped over, his too large encephalitic head and crossed eyes staring at you and wanting you to talk to him, and cousins Linda and Joan with their little-girl laughter, running around and giggling. After the first show we waited a long time for more test patterns to go away, then watched another show, and then went out to play.

I climbed their chinaberry tree to lie back on a branch and be alone and watch the clouds take on different shapes. Betty Ann was wild the rest of that day, as if her near-extinction hadn't fazed her. I looked down from my perch as she ran in her little-girl dress back to the house. And as I watched her open the door and disappear inside, I thought about it all again. The sudden recognition of her absence had felt like something had been dropped and would turn out to be broken. One moment she had been there, the next gone. It worried me, but it wasn't like it was a big worry. It was a worry I could think about only a little at a time, like trying to find something I know I can find if I look for it out of the corner of my eye, like locating a rabbit standing still in high grass.

And then Marvin called for me to come in. There was something really funny happening on television.

Forbidden Visit

I walk down the dirt path
from my house into the woods
and consider what I am doing.
In the twilight, as I step between the ruts,
crunching the sunburnt leaves of late September underfoot,
the tree frogs and crickets
announce the coming dark.
What do I know?
I am twelve.
Billy is only nine
and he has invited me for supper.

My parents would be nervous.
They don't approve of the Jenkins.
Shrimp fisherman
from the Gulf of Mexico
returning each year
in the off-season
to winter lodgings.
They cook outdoors,
sleep outside
more often than not.

The road curves.
I pass their camper.
Behind their rusty green and white GMC pickup,

their home emerges, unpainted
weathered wood,
three rooms,
a wooden porch,
and the worm bed underneath the house
fed by the kitchen sink.

I am curious.

Billy stares at me, excited,
from the wooden steps,
hand in his mouth.
He had worried I wouldn't come.

His dad is squatting by the firepit
at the end of the rutted drive
feeding the flames
with kindling and sticks.
He glances up at me but doesn't speak.
A night owl calls out.
Billy says, *He's here, Mom!*

His mom steps onto the porch
wiping her hands on an apron,
across her brow
a purple kerchief covering her head.

Billy's sister, barely thirteen,
rushes out the door,
around her mom,
down the stairs,

stands at the firepit
beside her father.
She's wearing a white dress
that falls straight from her shoulders,
twirling a strand of hair around her finger,
staring at me, wide-eyed.

Hi, I say.
She drapes her arm around her dad's neck.
Hi, she says.

Billy's mom welcomes me,
gestures to a chair in the family circle
near the fire.
The turtle caught in the Tombigbee
bubbles in a huge cast iron pot,
flames licking at its base.

Billy's dad sits down crossed-legged
on the ground
next to a blanket
spread with carvings:
a thin startled deer,
a runaway boy with his bindle stick,
an effigy of an aproned wife.
He picks up a block of dark wood,
firelight glinting from his knife,
wood shavings curling into the fire.
I am mesmerized
by the baying hound
emerging from the mahogany.

As the last of the day slips away,
his wife fills his tin cup with coffee.

I catch a glimpse of Billy's sister
across the flames.
Yesterday, she pulled me
down with her into the grass.
Arms wrapped around,
we touched each other all over
without speaking a word.
I had felt completely strange,
unmoored by the feel of her.

Now the only light is the fire
and I get to try for the first time
something I have only eaten from a can.
Holding its spiky green crown,
Billy's dad grabs a huge knife, machete-like,
uses four clean strokes
to cut off the rough brown rind
of a real pineapple.
Turning it on its side,
he slices the fruit just like that,
sweet, tart rings
for a bowl to share.
Billy's mom smiles at me.
I am amazed

by the fresh sweet taste,
by the whittled sculptures,

by the worms under the unpainted place,
and the extraordinary occasional neighbors,

feeling something about them
so vulnerable,
all civilization seems a threat.

The Large and Small of It
for Uncle Bud

...even the P-38s and the Flying Fortresses are as natural as
horse-flies;
  It is only that man, his griefs and rages, are not what they
seem to man, not great and shattering, but really

  Too small to produce any disturbance. This is good. This is
the sanity, the mercy. It is true that the murdered
Cities leave marks in the earth for a certain time, like fossil
rain-prints in the shale, equally beautiful.
  ~ Robinson Jeffers

*H*e lies in the hospital-white sheets, thinking of his land
      back home, of his lake, the weeds growing
around his apple orchard, the apples
      turning brown in the tall grasses.

Tomorrow, they say they will remove tumor, colon, and rectum.
      They say he will get used to the bag.
In a couple of months, he will not
      even notice it.

His wife's smiles are as sudden as the quail
      before his terror-filling footsteps.
She hears but she cannot see
      what he knows, knows and sees:
          the rotting brown-skinned apples
            bursting among the leaves.

A Day's Work

For so little pay
to move all day with that weight
slung backwards, and watch the dust
cover my hands like a new skin,
to stagger behind a black man who pulls
forward like a horse in harness,
so much power in his arms and back,
to lift that white substance from the plant,
that feeling of the seeds stuck in the center,
to stuff cotton balls in one smooth motion
without breaking stride
'til it's sundown beside the oak
beneath a red-varnished sky,
and an old man plopped down beside me,
wiping his eyes, face dust brown as mine,
saying, *Damn wind done made me cry.*

Choices
for Cindy

At seventeen, this is everything
it seems: the angry sound of your father's boots,
the silent uncertainty in the trees,
the open stubble covering the once-green fields,
pragmatic purple musk thistle
taking over the garden,
and the closed room
that holds the chemical smell
of your mother's sleep.

Of course you must run away
in the arms of a boy
with a fast car.

You take the path through the weeds.
But the fields of dead grasses
and the pine trees know the difference.
The crows sit in their branches, call and call
again. It is the same kind of madness
for them. They also, like galaxies,
travel in pairs. And they know,
better than most, the way things can go wrong.

Because your story
is only imagination and
the terrible bumping and grinding of trucks

hauling you and the kids
from one day into the next,
you choose to slash and burn
your own path through the forest,
surviving and blooming,
a radiant purple musk thistle,
thorns on all sides,
in a field of foxtails.

In Birmingham
for Annie Newton-Allison

Grandma is home from the hospital.
They couldn't kill her, she says, the way
they killed her son, Bud. The dead are so many
and so far behind.

She remembers the Depression, how Bud
had done the work of ten, not because he was stronger,
but because he was smarter, never wasted a thing
in his life. Dead, too, her husband who always wore
starched shirts because there were no excuses
before God, and her children who hadn't survived
childhood. It's everything and yet it's nothing.

She asks if we know about the caves near Bridgeport.
There are bones there, she's heard, artifacts
that go back two thousand years. She says she remembers
Birmingham before the streets were paved. It's everything
and yet it's nothing. In the backyard, she's had
a pecan planted to replace the fig. The tree
had worn itself out, she says, it had stopped
bearing fruit.

A Man

for Grandpa Curtis Allison

Dawn, and in this September morning, the old man watched the mists swirl thickly the length of his creek, the earth spongy and dark. He had walked a muddied path to the water's edge and then moved, a pale white figure clothed in Sunday black, through the mist toward the pasture and his bottom land. Out of the quiet came the occasional flat tone of a cow bell, one of his own. He walked without hurry. And with his staff, a thick dried vine he had cut for himself, he poked at the rotted timbers as he passed.

The old man came to a stop where the rotted logging bridge had stood. It lay collapsed under the water's swirl. The creek was high, backed up, foamy with scum. It seemed to flow in reverse. Brown, sawdust-colored froth gathered and circled on the surface. He turned and started around the flooded, muddied ground when a cottonmouth slipped from a limb off to his left.

The hushed wet slap of its body went through him like a chill. He stood for a moment and stared at the off-yellow shading just visible across its throat. Then he stepped over a deadfall and blocked its path to the creek.

A log on either side, the moccasin backed, then stopped and coiled. There was a hollow snapping noise. The mouth gaped open, displaying the white gullet. The old man stabbed at it with his staff. His eerie, high-pitched voice echoed briefly in the damp woods as he laughed.

When the snake lurched forward, the old man almost lost his footing, his white hair flapping down into his eyes. He stepped quickly to one side and his staff crashed heavily across the tail. The snake boiled immediately into a writhing mass that abruptly disappeared down the bank into the water.

The old man stared. Nothing. Rings widened across the surface, bent, then broke beneath the foam. Something else that would not be finished flared from inside him. Suddenly he was gasping. He could not get his breath. He staggered away from the water into a hollow of thorns and scrub. Then he sat down and stopped, leaned back against a mossed-over oak.

His eyes seemed unfocused, and yet in the twilight of this morning, hands by his side, he was still briefly alive in his life, as he watched the dragonflies before him mating in mid-air. And as he listened for the children running in his blood, he stared out through the rising mists at a glistening, pale white sun. For a moment it remained there, like something that was melting inside him. Then it was gone.

Let's Play a Game

from a story told of my grandfather

Say it was pretend, with a friend,
around 1890 or 1910,
and you've just come home
wearing your flannel shirt that's wet
along the cross of suspenders on your back.
      Your eyes are wide with shock.
      It was to be playing you were Jesse James
with your one-shot squirrel gun, and you've run
all the way home, leaving behind the sloping hill,
the thick grotto of trees growing up at an angle
to your sense of balance,
      leaving behind all those twisted dogwoods,
those Christ-crooked trees bursting green and white
and the one lone oak with your rope tied
just as it was supposed to be,
that grass brown rope
that was your birthday present
      around his neck so blue and bent
hanging from the tree
you'd decided was the hanging tree.

Grandmother Allison's Stance

My grandmother once told me that when going out in
public, I represent not just myself but the whole family.

After supper, stirring leftovers
into her cast iron pot:
ham hock, turnips, onion tops,
greens, okra, carrots
becoming our weekend soup.
A freshman in college,
I tell her about my classes.

She tells me about her mother
during the Depression,
an ignorant woman, she says.
And her grandfather,
a wanderer, a songwriter,
who left as a young man
but returned, old, to die,
his poems and stories
on the backs of paper bags.
Wasted words, said her mother,
and another mouth to feed.
Her mother burned them all.

Thick glasses, shoulders hunched,
greying waist-length hair
tucked on top in a bun,
she feels her way through her ordered house.
She stirs coals in the Glow Boy stove,

refills the water pan on top.
She readies my bed every evening,
turns back the hand-stitched quilts,
heavy and warmed.

Bedridden with pneumonia,
four sons at work,
all five daughters come
to rush her to the hospital,
to save her.
She intends to die at home, she says,
and if they don't agree
they can all just leave.
On the wall in her bedroom
remains a framed picture
cut from a National Geographic:
the winding Burma Road.

Parting

My father paced me as we shoveled
until I grew tired and watched him
watching me
shoveling
and then when I stopped
he grinned
his feet sinking slowly in the loose dirt
the sweat pouring down his muscled back
in streams.
Somehow he won then
and even as I packed my bags
our angry eyes clashing like iron
and I turned my back on him
I felt that smile
as he shoveled on
past all endurance
that strength of his arms and back
that unworded smile of his disappointment.

Non-Recouvrable: Unsalvageable
For Janice Kirkpatrick Entrekin
(1943-1966)

Riverside, Alabama

after F. Scott Fitzgerald

On the Coosa River, the newly damned water
backs up, becalmed and flat
against its banks. Riverside: one jail,
one sheriff, one police car.
Everything else is private property:
bait houses, restaurants, hot spots
of booze and easy women.

Call it what you will. Here
with the Coke bottles, beer cans,
bass plugs, hope is what was lost.
We go out for a midnight swim, step down
into warm water, know the ooze
of Coosa-buried forests
will suck us under.

No, love, the Coosa is nothing
like the Black Warrior. The Warrior
River still runs smoothly seaward
without a stop. Look there,
on the far bank, that house lit up in the fog.
Let's pretend it's yours,
or mine, or ours.

Holding the Invisible

Meaning,
holding those things which cannot be seen,
which I cannot show you,
the way a vase tilts inside me
when you walk by,
the way we live in each other's lives
as if it made no difference,
a breath of air,
the wind in the curtains,
the way we come together in the dark,
that feeling of something falling,
my out-stretched hands.

The Promised Land

*T*wo by two they enter in innocence,
believing everything they've heard
about high wire acts and safety-nets
and love, and keep their dreams
to themselves, like toys
defended from aggressors,
until one day in the kitchen,
an angry black eye of just-made coffee
swirls boiling into the cup,
and together they tear the cloth
of their understanding just where
it is most difficult to repair.

Night Song

At first it's the music
of her breathing, her song
of light rapture,
but, as from a darker source,
a bright pain fills her voice:
it becomes of speed,
of the necessity of broken bottles,
of whiskey and warm breath,
of the fight for Aristotle's unities
and symmetry and the river,
and the flowing into bottom lands.

After a Fight

*H*e enters her warm
and easy as night on a summertime
lake
          and afterwards, the covers
lift with the aroma of sex as his hands
drift over her shoulder and back,
and he feels something far away
become himself again, wonderfully calm,
home and close to sleep.

Ophelia's Dream, 1963

Love is whole only when love can be hurt,
she says as she spins
through a field
of dandelions and daisies,
her hands stretched out
like gifts of white gloves.

When she encounters before her
a glass brick house,
a door, a pane of glass
of no reflection,
she says,
The world is upright
at the cost of dreams,
as she walks the floor
of her madhouse waking.

How should I your true love know
From a former one?
From another one?
Why, by his cockle hat and staff,
And his sandal shoon.

And when the house bursts into flames
and the dead walk their broken parts in daylight
and the dust swells up into shapes she cannot face,
she says,

My dreams are larger than I willed.
Am I to blame for that?

And she smiles as she sings
and holds her fingers dripping with rainwater
against the wind.

The Photograph is Wrong

*I*t was on a chert-red road near Birmingham,
our weathered gray farmhouse tilting
toward the earth. Green fingers of kudzu
had claimed the chimney and roof.

When I look closely I can make out
railroad beds and a field of dead grass
in the distance. It was taken in Indian summer.
You are sitting under the mimosa trees, looking
like life has been good to you. It isn't true.

That was the year it snowed, a false spring
bloom on everything. I remember pointing to the trees,
saying how beautiful they were, undressed that way
and standing in ice.

Here in the Dark, Love

I'm out here in the dark, love,
because I wanted to be alone.
Because I wanted something to give in to.
I tried to remember how lives change,
alter and yet remain the same, but tonight
      I felt something break
as after a long fall. Now even our names
seem best left alone, unchanged
like names buried character by character
in stone.
      I remember the tunes, love,
that's why I've come. I remember
the honeysuckle touch of your tongue.
      You can see I'm here without my clothes,
and the moon's not bright, but listen to me first,
something's gone wrong in my life, some
things I've not told you about. Listen,
some blood always runs cold as mine.
This nakedness on the lawn
contains all I've ever been.
      I know you're going to say
I keep bringing you what has changed
without me.
      I know when I wake
in the morning, my seed will remain
one more secret egg on your plate,
but, you see, I don't care. I
do not know what has become of us.

This Unfinished Dream

You come to a small town in the South,
magnolias and crepe myrtle and an asylum
down the street, and there she stands.
Desire trembles inside you like a leaf
released in the wind.
Yes, I've been here before,
you think, directionless,
while she stands, aloof in the landscape,
rooted and yet free.
Sunlit, she shimmers in the breeze
like a princess tree in full bloom,
rich purple flowers fluttering
down her shoulders and spine.
When she turns to go you find
you are alone.
You follow ten steps behind.
The mayor, hanged from the limb of a nearby oak,
swings gently:
white suit, white shoes, and purple tongue,
and in the distance, kudzu climbs
a last green pine.
Life goes on
the way you knew it would, confused,
and now she waits without her clothes, waits
for you to know what she will not say,
there can be no escape,
and her image will hold you
bound as the blossoms at her feet.

Alabama Kudzu

*T*his is the fear, the words
trapped in the back of your throat,
that nothing is enough.
　　In your blood you trace
the inner latticework of kudzu,
you understand the brown trees,
all motion pulled to the ground,
like horses drowned in quicksand,
the tall and crumbling pine
beneath an undying green.
　　But this is only the fear.
You have told yourself, regret nothing.
Your eyes are still blue and inside
you are still capable of surrendering.

Advantage

In France beside some shabby old wall
the water runs dirty with sunlight
and I walk, moss-brown stones beneath my feet,
toward you with open arms. You are blond now.
You have changed only the color of your hair.
All the rest remains the same.

In your eyes I see you don't understand,
as if you're puzzled by my greeting. Being polite
you invite me to coffee before finding you're afraid:
there are no witnesses. Always we are alone.
It's then you begin to doubt, and I discover
once again how your grave face will unravel

remembering when we were young,
when your dark hair glistened like a river in the sun.

Asylum

Whereof one cannot speak,
thereof one must be silent.
    —*Ludwig Wittgenstein*

Coming into her moonlight
I immediately forgot where I was,
wandered about in the backyard
of my dreams, found myself

unable to go inside the house,
for no reason, like an animal
confused by a strange new fence
that made no sense,

that blocked the only way home,
and I sat down in those winter-dried leaves,
feeling memory suddenly opening before me,
a life turning inside out,

the way she blushed in her bones,
long hair flowing over her face, fading away
in midnight air, descending stairs,
and me outside my soul, undressed and cold.

To Remember You

I have to let in all the light
I can bear,
and it's still not enough.

Over the years you have been erasing
all traces of yourself,
pulling everything into the ground
behind you.

Once I believed in you
the way I believed in maps
and the way home. I was wrong.

The seasons proceed,
and we reach inside each other,
begin living in a new kind
of weather.

You live now only in my most inward life,
spread out, like pieces of shell at the shore.

Fourteen Reasons Why

1.
The grandmother hated men,
had since she was sixteen
and discovered what it was
men always wanted.

2.
The mother couldn't stand the grandmother,
had married, conceived, and divorced
in less than a month
of misunderstandings.

3.
And then they were three.

4.
And the mother worked
and the grandmother stayed home,
and their little girl became a devout Baptist.

5.
The men rarely stayed overnight,
except on weekends.

6.
The mother was once Queen
of the high school dance.

7.
The grandmother was always overweight,
dipped snuff and drank on the sly.

8.
Their little girl made straight A's,
sang and helped conduct the high school choir.
9.
The mother married again,
two weeks before her daughter's wedding.
10.
Their little girl married
a bright young English major.
11.
Their little girl's first lesbian experience
occurred only a few days
before her marriage.
12.
Their little girl committed suicide
two years later.
She stepped in front of a car
one bright day
after a beautiful snowfall in Tennessee.
13.
It was her third try that worked.
14.
Her note read:
Forgive me.
Je suis non-recouvrable.

The Fish Found in Her Dream

The bird, dark and mean, crosses the creek,
lands on the prow of an old boat.
Her feathers turn purple in the sun.
Her call falls like a stone.
        I wish it were not so,
but this is how we meet.
When the bird calls, I always come.
I feel her dark joy congealing like blood,
her dreams changing my arms into wings.
I glide with her, alive.
I dive and devour
what shines beneath her in the stream.
        But no sooner does she come
than she's gone,
leaving the taste of her gift
dying in my throat.
I am left empty,
the place where she dreams.

Alabama Night Walk

In every direction is a creek.
Farther back, in the woods,
there is a swamp, wild magnolia trees,
the heavy scent of honeysuckle.
These woods are a part of you.
      No traffic, no streetlights, no sidewalk.
The sound of your footsteps
on the asphalt
echoes in the night.
      You came back
because you were born here.
Your first wife is buried here.
Tree frogs, crickets, the sound of owls
hunting in the dark.
The woods are never far away in Alabama.
      On the left, someone's dog barks.
On the right, the house of a cousin
who tells how you can't trust
the government, doctors, or priests.
In this neighborhood, all dreams are the same:
failure is a sin, somebody's ill,
everyone's hungry and you can't hunt the deer.
      Clear as the moonlight on the pavement,
you no longer belong here.
Your family loves you.

They pray for you.
       Now deep down
you know how kindness kills,
how kudzu is a Southern kind of snow,
how, as soon as you leave,
everything will grow obscure again.

The Meaning of Escape

Alabama Politics
(19 Ways of Seeing the Southern Strategy)

*Don't force me by law, by statute, by Supreme Court
decision...to cross over in those intimate things where
I don't want to go. Let me build my life. Let me have
my church. Let me have my school. Let me have
my friends. Let me have my home. Let me have my
family. And what you give to me, give to every man in
America and keep it like our glorious forefathers made
– a land of the free and the home of the brave.*

> –Rev. W.A. Criswell (1956), leader of the conservative
> Southern Baptist Convention, in response to *Brown
> v.Board of Education*, rhetoric which became a
> primary political weapon of the culture wars.

1.
All the clocks are melting.

2.
Alabama Democratic Governor George Wallace
makes a *Stand in the Schoolhouse Door:*
Segregation now.
Segregation tomorrow.
Segregation forever.

3.
JFK is assassinated in Dallas.

4.
Designated successor LBJ
passes the Civil Rights Bill
and the Voting Rights Act.

5.
White terrorists bomb
the 16th Street Baptist Church in Birmingham,
killing four black children.
6.
Martin Luther King
is invited to lead a peaceful protest
because *Injustice is here.*
7.
MLK pens *Letter from a Birmingham Jail:*
Perhaps it is easy
for those who have never felt
the stinging darts of segregation
to say, 'Wait.'
8.
A philosophy grad student's child
is born in Birmingham.
9.
His wife commits suicide.
10.
The grad student quits school,
moves home,
takes to his bed,
doesn't get up.
11.
His mother is sick,
but has to care
for her new grandchild.
12.
His father is an apolitical Dixiecrat,
a Methodist who rarely goes to church,

a moonshine maker,
a party drinker.

13.
When the grad student's despair lifts,
he has a full beard.

14.
His father is dismayed.

15.
The grad student
becomes a teacher for Head Start
in an all-black neighborhood.

16.
His father disowns him
as *a traitor to his race,*
throws him out of the house.

17.
The grad student takes his little boy
to start a new life
in California.

18.
Time begins again.

19.
His father votes
for Richard Milhous Nixon.

Leaving Alabama

What I hide from myself
I have begun to know.
Like an umbrella
left behind in the rain.
A blossoming azalea
bends its new December flower
against the basement window.
It grows inappropriately pink,
suicidal in unseasonable heat.

Off-kilter, in my father's house,
the present is not my own.
His idle lawnmower
smells of oil and gas,
his red tool chest still locked.

I stand in the window, thinking
of this false Spring's offerings,
Don't believe it. Oh, go back. Wait, wait,
and the wind moves
through the blossoming trees, whispering
to the leaves to be still, quiet,
in words like *dreaming and sleep.*

Sound of rain accumulates
and the gutters overflow,

water drips past me,
the confused sounds of a world
crying out like croaking frogs.

Pine, oak, ironwood, birch, apple trees
and the ground still wet
spongy, umber brown.
Last year, a sudden freeze,
dead red leaves lining the ground,
a clean winter kill.
It is time for me to go.

Report from Thomas,
Ten Years After the Accident
for Birmingham Southern friends Dwight and Jon

1.
In the humid steel-mill air,
dirt of Birmingham, Alabama,
with the taste of beer
in the back of my throat
I watched him start again
how that last time he'd witnessed
a white flash of himself
leaving his body.

2.
The doctor had taken him off
shock therapy, he remembered,
but no one told the nurse,
and she refused to listen.

3.
The only fair result, he whispered,
should end with her murder.

4.
In his dreams, he said,
lately he recalls the vision
of his already dead friend
beneath the car,
and how he'd promised him enough pain
to make a difference, to appease the suffering
of his dying. But it hadn't worked.

5.
He knew why, he said,
and looked me in the eye:
because Occurrence precedes Essence.
But he'd figured it out too late.
Now he was forced to write things down
to keep his reasoning straight.
6.
Everyone has the right to be unique, he's decided,
and that's why he's against reincarnation. It was
a kind of body stealing, or worse, and when he died
he would refuse to come back. He would lie there
with the universe, he said, and rot.
7.
Now that it was too late, he told me, he would like
to go back to school. The first time through, his
education didn't take.
8.
Thought that seeing that white flash of one's self
was a sure sign of an inferior personality.
9.
Believed his best liked reason for anything was
Einstein's thirteenth reason for the General Theory
of Relativity, that it was personally satisfying.
10.
Wished Tillich in *The Courage to Be* hadn't fallen back
on technical language to explain the tough parts. After
reading it again, he said, he felt he hadn't understood
something really important to know.

11.

Laughed when the bartender came up to us to ask if
he could just stand there and listen, and would we
like another drink on the house.

12.

Allowed as how he was sorry, really there was nothing
more could be said, and stood up and shook my hand
and returned to a world we'd not spoken of.

For Sena

Whose dad had died
before she was born,
who made all A's
until Chemistry.
She flunked it one summer,
the first black mark, ever,
on her record,
I'll do better this winter,
she said, and flunked again.
And laughing strangely,
failed it again in the Spring.
        The campus joke, all A's
and three F's, who finally
took Geology; claimed she'd
best discover the lay of the land.
        I remember her
thin, long-limbed,
all those sudden smiles,
the day she ran off with a man
not right in his head,
and the quality of her answers,
no matter
what was asked of her.

Letter from my Father

Let what comes come.
Let what goes go.
Find out what remains.
> — *Ramana Maharshi (1879-1950)*

I told you the beans needed weeding,
and while you're at it,
pick the ripe okra.

Marvin deserved his beating,
I know he weeded all the Johnson grass,
but he also chopped down all the corn.

Well, maybe I was wrong
about the whipping.
But he got over it.

Your brother is hard-headed,
he won't listen. I know
you got upset, always the *sensitive one.*

Nobody ever cut me any slack.
I built the house.
I poured the foundation by myself.

Your beautiful mother was ill.
I went to work,
I paid the bills for all eight of us.

You were lazy, a dreamer,
a college degree
one of your crazy schemes,

sitting around,
sitting in,
avoiding work.

In spite of the fights,
we had good times,
vacations, white beaches,

Panama City,
we played on Gulf Shores,
rubbed lotion on the sunburn,

we took care of each other.
Just know that I loved you,
and I loved your mother.

Remember
when you left us to go West,
back to school, you betrayed us.

But I was the one
drove the forty miles
from Birmingham to Tuscaloosa

to give you
the hundred dollars,
to say goodbye.

Dear Jordi（Tuscaloosa, Alabama）

*L*isten, love, the town I grew up in
is behind me,
as well as that woman
who killed herself.
I would have left her
anyway, eventually.

Sure, we'll always come back,
don't I know it,
to that place
that we can't leave behind,
that gave us
the names of things
we take with us.

We take on that shape
we discover
inside each other.

Stay? It's easy to say.
No matter.
The river runs on
without us.

Listen, love, it's what's best
for the both of us.
Already I feel
that sun rising
on the Eastern horizon,
and it seems these dreams
are like imaginary cups of gold
tipped over and spilled out
like slow shadows.

Birmingham

for Cynthia Wesley, Carole Robertson,
Addie Mae Collins, and Denise McNair

Of all the places you could die
trapped if you didn't leave fast
or have lots of money, this is the one
you remember best. This is your birthplace.
    You wanted out the day she ran away,
left you, the child, and the furniture.
But you stayed, innocent and twenty-one,
made love to practiced women. One,
forty-one, who kept your child for free;
one, thirty-three, who hoped her husband
died, a little at a time; and one,
twenty-nine, who came to you animalized,
hardened with lies.
    It was a steel-time town, younger
and harder than Birmingham Sunday could break.
Four black children died. You made love
to the wife of a salesman. He failed
to give her children. And failed again:
she cried when you stopped cold,
told her, *no, no more children.*
    That night outside Memphis, the Mississippi
mosquitoes like Furies bidding you goodbye,
you turn in your mind the meaning of escape.
Almost, you wanted to lie, you're innocent
if you don't go back. The child asleep, your red car
packed, you douse the fire and drive out fast.

Desert-Wrecked Dreamer:
California

One Day at a Time

It is easy enough
being sick of one's self,
to fear breaking open
when you least expect it,
when you are afraid of sleep
and eating lunch every day.

Sometimes an emptiness
must be constructed
inside you, again,
one day at a time,
creating a vacuum
from the absence
of what surrounds you,

a vacuum that knows
only of itself
and the bones
that are left behind,
that absorbs even light.
That's the place
where something new
can be born.

High, All-night Driving to Berkeley

Summer, 1967: I'm 26, a widower with a three-year-old son and $400. Go west, my philosophy professor advises, go to Berkeley. That's where it's happening.

Drink beer, follow the headlights,
the highway knows where a woman waits
who loves me. Drunks pass on by;
all maniacs stay in bed; I'm high
and Berkeley's near with its strong
ocean-like ways. The desert behind, a song
plays in my ear. Already sea waves run white
lines one at a time down the moon-lit night.
Your tides pull me along; your curve of thigh
runs in my mind; your round brown eyes
close once again. *Take me, take me,* says the song;
the maps show I can make no wrong
decisions. Home, to know your body as before;
I am a desert-wrecked dreamer come to shore.

Flashback
For Janice

In San Francisco the surf pounds
and I stand quite still,
the shaking of the car now inside me.
And I remember her walking toward the highway
to Memphis, her back and shoulders bent forward
into her gray unreasonableness,
the hard edge of her gentle denials:
only going out to be alone, alone
for a walk, for a walk by herself,
and surely I could understand.

It was over twenty years ago.
She was not coming back. She was leaving,
wearing her smiles and refusals,
her firmness after so many failures.
And still my dumb hands wanted
to hold her, but she peeled them loose,
and it was snowing, and there were
large wet flakes on her face.

It was the beginning of winter.
I wasn't ready, I was outside my body
looking down into the dark green
watercress under the culvert,
a thin film of ice covered the roads,
and I remember seeing myself standing there,
rush-hour traffic backed up for miles,
her note folded in my hand.

There was nothing I could have said.
She wasn't there. She was nowhere, pale and still,
lost in the silence of the snowfall,
in the cold air, gone, the flash of a leaping fish
in the distance.
          And I remember how it was, floating
up above the cars and trucks, weightless
over the old country road, and nothing to be done,
only me, the phone man's son, floating
in the slow flood of an evening light,
the policemen waving everyone on, the flashing
red lights over her stark white face,
and no answers as I floated on,
between lives,
          between then and now,
here on an early winter's day, standing
beside the Great Highway,
just south of the Cliff House, remembering,
watching as the sun is suffused
with magenta and orange,
that indifferent engine of light, magnificent
as it turns below the waves.

At Hearst Street House, Berkeley

For Caleb and Demian

"Trouve avant de chercher (Find before seeking)."
~Paul Valéry

It was night. My new life
wandered outside on the sidewalk
in the dark. I watched as it stopped,
stared inside, a reflection in the glass.
Nothing was clear, but I could see
the new shape outlined in the grass
in the rain, going nowhere, hazy, like
moonlight refracted in fog.

Behind me, a yellow lamp,
a child's picture of a many-colored room,
orange and silver and gold. Each wall
a different color. The family slept on.

But something was wrong,
a drop had occurred in the atmosphere,
a permanent change in the weather,
and whatever life I had lived before
I would never live again.

January, The Day You Died

for Janice

Back and forth to work
reading *Wuthering Heights,*
on the bus with Catherine
and Heathcliff, umbrellas,
five o'clock faces and I see,
I see you in the street,
wine-colored skirt, blue tennis sneakers,
stepping from the curb
past the corner of my eye, horns,
and the open door, rush-hour traffic.
Everywhere wet hair,
the black ordinary coats,
a flower store. Never there.
A small dog barks. Distant.
A trick of the mind to see you today
in California, so many years into darkness,
and under the awning, standing
beside a can of white, gold-centered
daisies, I no longer ask why. Rain
dances the sidewalks. It's Wednesday.
We have nothing to say.

November in Berkeley
for Gail

*T*he back door,
hanging by its heels,
swings open
and it's November again.
    Outside, Pittosporum berries,
orange and whiskey-scented,
have fallen to the ground.
But there will be no snow,
no bears in the driveway,
and no frozen pond, its murky waters
gone veined and milky as glass.
    It's good the way we invent what we need,
catering our lives with beginnings and endings,
the way I look backwards wearing disasters
on my sleeve while you plan ahead,
search for joy in every potted plant, and
it's as if here,
where winter never really comes,
    we have learned
to rely on our inner clocks
and let the seasons
reach inch by inch
into the soil of ourselves.

New Year's Day, 1983

My sister on the phone from Birmingham
with my mother who can no longer talk
but who listens and tries to be well,
and my dad who announces his retirement
like success,

> and suddenly
> I remember him from before,
> before he and I stopped speaking for four years,
> before my mother began her long descent into Parkinson's,

> before Birmingham Sunday tore me loose from my roots,
> and all the deaths, and the dying,

> *my father, on my bicycle, on his way back*
> *from his first day at work after the war,*

this unworded man, his new laughter,
wishing me a Happy New Year.
And somehow it is,
and, in this moment,
we are everything
we set out to be.

What the Woman Said in my Dream

It's true that time alters everything
into something less and that's a fact,
she said, but think of Spring
and how a river shakes loose the freeze
from its banks.

Perhaps it's time you go back,
release the things you've trapped,
the wind in the empty Mason jars
on your shelf.

But I thought of the buttons
missing down the front of my shirt,
and of another's eyes on the coming snow
on the horizon, and I knew somehow
that only absence would be found
of what I had left behind.

Thoughts from a Plane Over Birmingham

My mother sick, the plane drifts
years, banking for landing, and suddenly
I'm home,
    and the orange, industrialized sky
still says the furnaces are working overtime,
steel from the steel-born town.
    The stewardess shakes the sleepers awake,
the engines rev, landing gear down, and the home
I thought I'd left behind
returns as we touch the ground. Home
    because what opens at the beginning
remains open till the end.

Renouvellement:
Renewal

Alabama in December

1.

First day back, Birmingham, in the dark basement
of my father's house, standing below ground
looking up: old Mason jars,
opaque Coca-Cola bottles, one window;
outside in this too warm December,
the newly budding pink of azalea blossoms.
And I can still feel my mother's hand
from early morning, shaking,
the children afraid of her now,
her closeness to death, dark veins
tracking the dry swamp of her skin,
shaking.

In a thin winter sweater, I wander outside
under the close Southern sun,
my feet walking my father's land,
feel again the way pine, oak,
ironwood form a stand,
the ground gone a dusty ochre
brown, dead red leaves
holding forth from a single tree.

Footprints. Relatives in every direction.
Like creeks, rivers, graves:
this family.

2.

Afternoon, in the dim bedroom light,
I watch as her shaking stops
and starts her staring, far off
into a world of her own, all bones
and soft transparent flesh. As she drifts,
her thin arms move, hands grip at the bed
as if to take hold once again the edge
of her bridge back before sleep.

In the quiet dark I remember playing
in Red Mountain's forests and mines,
how we invented ways out,
nightmares climbing up behind us
out of the muck, and the white sightless fish
we found, trapped in the iron-red water
of an underground lake.

And later, like a plane leaving the ground,
I remember those curving shapes, those blind
creatures suddenly visible in our light,
as real as the gentle bed of lilies she grew one year,
as real as the life we shared,
and yes, that was happy,
that life, when I could walk all the way home
with my eyes closed.

Dink

I know a man who, at birth,
was broken by a doctor whose hands
faltered in the too long and too hard delivery.
   He grew up broken, his eyes crossed,
his legs withered, his head too large in circumference,
and his whole back scarred from neck to hip.
   He was given one year, two, ten, and now he's thirty,
cousin Dink, with a grade school education,
without bitterness, with scars on his too often burned legs
that have no feeling, and
       would I send him a drinking glass,
the kind you buy at tourist spots, or if not that,
perhaps a road map of California?

All That Remains Is her
Inlaid Mozart Music Box

I remember my mother
playfully opening her cupped hands,
revealing a butterfly inside,
orange and yellow and black.
Surprise! Suddenly it was there,
full of color and imagined eyes,
before it took flight and was gone.

While I play on the back porch
with my baby brother
at my mother's sister's house,
Mom runs the clothes
through the ringer washer
and hangs them on the line.
We push the stroller
down the back alley
to the park,
to the corner store.

Dad came home from the War.
I was on my own
at four, evicted and alone.
He closed the door
to my mother's room.
She was still a force,
deliberate and delicate,
never raised her voice,

danced in slow motion
through my life,
through the whirlwind of my siblings
coming and going,
arriving one after the other,
my mother slipping away from me.
I learned to read to be on my own.

Sitting alone in our backyard
in Alabama in the fall,
still a pretty woman,
green gardening gloves,
shaking hands in her lap,
glass of iced tea nearby
dripping on the old stone wall,
kudzu vines
beside the woodbine and nightshade.
She knows she is dying,
will soon have to
leave us behind,
an angry man
and six children to care for.

At my mother's side,
Dad told me it was time to let her go.
About the plastic flowers, he said,
as he placed them beside her bed,
These will stay beautiful forever.

Dulled hospital faces roll
like felled trees
along the backs of couches.

I try to speak,
but words clutter the hallway.
There is nothing to say.

Everywhere, the weather feels the same,
a bleached sky before Spring,
a dissolution just beginning.

Where was I going
in such a hurry
while she called my name?

April in Alabama

*for Betty Ruth Allison-Entrekin (1920-1986), who
died after a 15-year battle with Parkinson's Disease*

My father once shouted that she loved me best.
Now, again he stares without seeing, and yes,
I know he thinks I have her feel on me still.
Always she was so quiet, insisting without speaking,
always seeming to know she gave context, shape,
thickness to things.

And now her relations have arrived, her grandchildren,
dressed up, stage-whispery voices, this
quiet sobbing punctuating the sunny morning,
with a pack of Marlboros left on an end table,
coffee, truck roars from a nearby freeway,
and me, just in from California, like an unholy
ear, listening.

In chapel we sit with silent faces, the dark
mahogany walls closing in. The hoarse cough
of a relative with a cold, echoes.

And now my cousin Rodney, no longer a boy
but a Mississippi preacher taking hold, speaks
and the background rush of our lives floats away
as the sound of his voice spreads over us,
honeyed and slow, *I remember times we'd come to comfort her,
worried and concerned, but she'd smile and say, year after year,*

'Go your way, there's nothing you can do here,
Go your way . . .'

Outside, a casket winds past the new chapel,
the gravesides, and in the distance, kudzu
clings to the new leaves. Spring. Still Alabama
forests remain a muddy, monochromatic brown.
What stirs is the new, busy noisiness in the humid air,
of wasps and dirt-daubers at their nests.

With everyone gone, like wind
I feel her out there, like fish and mosquitoes,
lakes, blowing grass and dead leaves, dung beetles,
bees. Yet there is an emptiness in the landscape
as when the dogwoods are in full bloom and no one notices,
a sadness like oil cans and abandoned shacks, empty stores
beside the highway. Spirits that no one knows.

Postcard View, Panama City

*H*aving come back
to seaside evening tides,
I stand beside the Gulf of Mexico and watch
as ominous clouds rise on the horizon.
They sit poised like participants as we wade out
chest deep in the surf, brave emerald green waves
under magentas and distant pinks high in the sky.
Dad and I, alone, awkwardly together, try to talk
over high winds and quickening surf,
too loud, and no desire anyway,
for a real colloquy.

I remember him younger, angrier,
beating my brother with a belt,
when his dark handsome face
turned alien as an insect's.
We all feared him, his cold face, his sudden rages,
that force that flew toward us,
unconcerned with outcomes,
and we ran, tried to hide with our stories, in closets,
tried to remove him from the pages of our lives.

Now I am taller and Dad is much smaller.
Another wave smacks him in the face
and he laughs, embarrassed.
On a whim, I remember as I edge deeper,
he doesn't know how to swim.

Drucilla

1.

My father has remarried.
He is in love.
She enters our house,
younger than Dad,
commands ownership of the room.
Alluringly thin-waisted, yet
sturdy, my new stepmother always carries
a pearl-handled pistol in her purse.
A dead shot, she proclaims.
If attacked by a man,
she plans to aim low.

Dad rewrites our history,
talks proudly
of the rough love
of our early years,
leaves out the beatings,
leaves out the random slaps
to the back of my head.
A random enforcer of order,
more quick to strike than to find out why.

He never speaks of Mother.
Her inlaid music box of Mozart

sits on his new wife's dresser
amidst her lacquered sea shells
and bric-a-brac.

2
His sibilant whisper
seeps over the line,
three thousand miles away
in his assisted-living facility.

She left me because I'm impotent,
eighty-six, in phlegmatic breaths,
She loaded up all the furniture,
and so I asked her, 'Where you going?'
She said, 'I'm leaving you.'
I said, 'Fine. Don't come back.'

Outside my window in California,
I stare down into the green
of Yuba River Canyon.
Dru had fed him Benadryl
until the doctors explained
it was causing his strokes.
The bank accounts closed,
the gold coins missing,
the money gone,
everyone whispered,
She knew what she was doing.

I say, *Do you miss her?*

Last Parting
Remlap, Alabama

Asleep in his air-conditioned room
face bathed in black and white TV light
he aspirates something from supper,
and wakes unable to breathe.
Old pneumonia takes hold,
hours of fighting for air,
hyperventilating in the cold,
before the ambulance arrives
before his heart gives out
lungs collapse, kidneys fail.

But machines resuscitate him
breathe for him, pump blood,
track erratic brain waves
until Marvin says,
unplug him.

Against all medical predictions,
he struggles on, breathes on his own,
fights for three days and three nights.

He was terribly strong, Marvin says.

But that was all, I thought,
the best of what he gave us.

Azaleas
for Charles Edward Entrekin, Sr. (1919-2006)

I sail over the causeway
flying across water and time
through the scent of salt sea air
past sand dunes and sea oats
to the bright white driveway
of my father's last house.
Inside is a Formica table,
an old oak chair.
Across its solid bent back
hangs a faded work shirt,
red and black plaid,
the shirt he wore in the garden
of string beans, okra and elephant ears.
In time, when I try it on,
the shirt comes apart in tatters.
I will bury it under the pine duff
next to my azaleas.

Renewal

My father's words survive like weeds
around my stepping stones.
You were always the one, he spat at me
one Alabama summer,
an angry emptiness, another caesura,
between us, another landmine
I can't disarm.

I was his eldest.
I stepped over him.
I ignored him.

He loved me. He loved me not.

I didn't go to his funeral,
a mistake. As Faulkner said,
The past is never dead.
It's not even past.

Author Biography

Charles Entrekin was born in 1941 in Birmingham, Alabama. He took his B.A. in English from Birmingham Southern College in 1964. He left Birmingham in 1965 and lived in various states (New York, Tennessee, Alabama, and Montana) while pursuing advanced degrees in philosophy and creative writing.

Charles Entrekin holds an MFA in Creative Writing and founded the Creative Writing department at John F. Kennedy University and the Berkeley Poets Workshop & Press. Currently he is editor of the e-zine Sisyphus, (https://sisyphuslitmag.org) a magazine of literature, philosophy and culture, and managing editor of Hip Pocket Press (www.hippocketpress.com).

Charles is the author of six previous books of poetry: *The Art of Healing*, with Gail Entrekin, (Poetic Matrix Press, 2016); *Listening: New & Selected Work*, (Poetic Matrix Press, 2010); *In This Hour*, (BPW&P, 1990); *Casting for the Cutthroat & Other Poems*, (BPW&P, 1986); *Casting for the Cutthroat*, (Thunder City Press, 1978); *All Pieces of a Legacy*, (BPW&P, 1975). Charles' novel, *Red Mountain: Birmingham, Alabama, 1965*, was published in May, 2008, by El Leon Literary Arts (www.elleonliteraryarts.org).

CPSIA information can be obtained
at www.ICGtesting.com
Printed in the USA
FSHW020634190920
73589FS